UK employr

Homewc

Bullet Points

email: robin@worklaw.co.uk
website: htttps://www.worklaw.co.uk
telephone: 07549 168 675

© Robin Hawker
All rights reserved

this edition: September 2020

ISBN: 9798678674265
Imprint: Independently published

UK Employment Law
Bullet Point Booklets

1. Disciplinary Procedures
2. National Minimum Wage
3. Employment Contracts
4. Defending Employment Tribunal Claims
5. TUPE
6. Staff Handbooks
7. Disability Discrimination
8. Settlement Agreements
9. Redundancy
10. Recruitment
11. Sick Pay
12. Maternity
13. Homeworking (this booklet)

Disclaimer

This series of booklets is titled *UK employment law*. This is not an entirely accurate title. The focus is on the law of England and Wales. Employment laws in Scotland and Northern Ireland are broadly the same as in England and Wales but may differ occasionally.

Employment law is complex and changes frequently due to political, social and economic pressures, and the law might have changed by the time you read this booklet: the publication date is on the title page.

Please view this booklet as a brief, *bullet-pointed* guide to employment law. It is not a complete guide. You must not rely on this booklet for anything other than a brief overview of the law and procedures: our attempt to simplify the law might cause misunderstanding and ambiguities.

This booklet does not—and cannot—cover everything. For example, where bullet-point lists are given they may be incomplete as only more common items might be listed.

You are advised to consult a specialist in employment law to answer specific questions.

Homeworking

It is advisable for an employer to have at least 2 documents for a homeworker:

- a **Homeworking Employment Contract**; and
- a separate **Homeworking Policy**; or, (instead of a separate Homeworking Policy)
- a section in a Staff Handbook which relates to homeworking and contains the same information as in a Homeworking Policy.

The Homeworking Employment *Contract* should contain only those terms which are necessarily contractual, such as pay and holiday entitlement.

The Homeworking *Policy* should contain non-contractual rules and procedures relating to homeworking, such as how often the homeworker is expected to change their computer login password.

A change to homeworking

An employer can change an Employment Contract only if the employee agrees to the change, otherwise the employer risks an employment tribunal claim.

An employer can (with less risk of an employment tribunal claim) change a Policy document or a Staff Handbook, providing they act fairly and reasonably in doing so.

The terms and conditions of an existing employee's contract of employment will need to be changed to reflect the fact that they will now work from home.

However, an employee working from home must not be treated less favourably than an employee working from business premises, otherwise the difference in treatment might give rise to employment tribunal claims, such as for discrimination.

The change to working from home will not cause a break in the employee's continuous period of employment.

For existing employees, the necessary changes to their Employment Contract should be set out in a new employment contract or in a written notice of variation to their existing employment contract. Basic terms and conditions of employment covering matters such as:

- pay;
- holidays;
- pension.

will probably remain the same.

However, other terms and conditions will need to be changed, deleted or added to reflect homeworking, such as, for example:

- workplace address;
- flexible working hours;
- a right to the employer to check that the home is suitable.

Assuming that the job role is suitable for home working, employers will need to consider matters such as (the list is not exhaustive):

- how to monitor work done;
- the provision of necessary equipment for work;
- dedicated internet and telephone lines;

- health and safety in the home;
- data security and confidentiality in the home;
- any insurance required to cover working from home;
- whether homeworking is prohibited by a mortgage or a lease or a restrictive covenant.

Basically, employees who work from home will remain subject to the same contractual obligations as colleagues who work from the employer's business premises with varied or added contractual terms applicable to homeworking.

Tax

There will be tax implications if:

- the employer allows the homeworker to use Company equipment for *personal* use, or
- if the employer pays or contributes towards the employee's *household* expenses.

If employers provide equipment, services and supplies to an employee who works from home, and allows the employee personal use of such equipment, the element of personal use is likely to attract tax unless the personal use is insignificant.

For a household expense to be tax deductible, the expense must be incurred wholly, exclusively and necessarily in the performance of the duties of employment.

There is a limit to the amount that employers can contribute to the employee's household expenses without their contribution attracting tax.

The limits for 2020/2021 are £6.00 a week if employees are paid weekly or £26 a month for employees paid monthly.

An amount greater than £6 each week might be approved by HMRC if there is evidence to justify it.

Apart from the weekly limit referred to above, if the payments the employer makes are more than the employee's additional household expenses they count as earnings, and the employer must work out the excess and add this amount to the employee's gross earnings. Employers should refer to HM Government website:

https://www.gov.uk/expenses-and-benefits-homeworking

And also refer to HMRC's website:

https://www.gov.uk/hmrc-internal-manuals/employment-income-manual/eim32815

Notes

Note 1: The draft Homeworkers Employment Contract in this booklet is drafted on the basis that the employer does not permit personal use of equipment provided to the employee, and does not pay or contribute towards extra household expenses attributable to working from home.

Note 2: If the employer choses to permit personal use and/or pay or contribute towards extra household expenses, they should confirm any such arrangement in a separate document signed by both parties. The draft Homeworkers Employment Contract in this booklet will also need to be amended to reflect the arrangement.

Note 3: Until the end of the 2020-21 tax year, there is a temporary exemption from income tax and NICs for expenses reimbursed by an employer to an employee where the expenses are incurred on the purchase of equipment obtained for the "sole purpose" of enabling the employee to work from home due to the 2019 novel coronavirus epidemic (Covid-19).

Note 4: Both employers and employees should take advice from tax accountants in regard to the tax implications of 'personal use' and 'household expenses'.

Insurance

The employer must ensure that their compulsory Employers' Liability Insurance covers employees working at home.

The employer should also ensure that equipment they provide to the homeworker is adequately insured, particularly against damage and theft.

Alternatively, the employer should check that the homeworker has adequate insurance cover for the employer's equipment.

The employer should ensure that the employee's home is reasonably secure. If it is considered insecure the employer should consider whether to install a burglar-alarm system and stronger locks.

Business use of premises

Homeworkers should check that they are not restricted by the freehold or lease of the property, or the terms of their mortgage or tenancy agreement, from using their home for business purposes. It might be necessary to obtain the permission in writing of the employee's bank, building society or landlord to work from home.

Health and Safety

An employer has statutory and common law duties regarding the health, safety and welfare at work of all its employees (including its employees working from home) and to provide and maintain a safe working environment, safe equipment and safe systems of work, and to provide necessary training.

These health and safety duties mean that the employer must carry our periodic risk assessments, including in the homeworker's home. For example, as with all employees who work with computer monitors, homeworkers should be given eye tests.

Disabled employees

An employer's duty to make reasonable adjustments in relation to a disabled person also applies to a homeworker. Therefore, if the employee is disabled, the employer should visit their home for the express purpose of checking whether reasonable adjustments can and should be made in the home to assist the employee in their work.

Benefits for employees

The reasons for the popularity of homeworking with employees are obvious;

- employees with children can look after them and avoid

- expensive child-minding fees;
- no commuting to work;
- some find it easier to concentrate at home;
- etc.

Homeworking is not popular with all employees;
- some miss being in the office;
- some find it more difficult to concentrate at home;
- etc.

Benefits for employers

Homeworking is becoming popular with a significant number of employers.

The benefits of homeworking to employees include;
- reduced need to provide office space;
- employees available to spend more time working instead of commuting;
- etc.

However, for various reasons not all employers are happy with homeworking and want all their staff back in the workplace.

Employment contract for a homeworker

You may use the draft contract below in your business.

An editable copy in RTF format can be downloaded from: https://worklaw.co.uk/homeworkers.html.

However, please remember that the document was not drafted specifically for your business and may not be entirely suitable for your business. Probably it will need amending.

Worklaw (https://worklaw.co.uk/employmentcontracts.php) can draft a Homeworking Employment Contract and a Homeworking Policy specifically for your business, for a total fee of £198.

This fee also includes advice on employment law by email or telephone for one month from the date we received payment of our fee.

This document (or a document similar to the one below, which complies with Section 1 of the Employment Rights Act 1996, as amended by The Employment Rights (Employment Particulars and Paid Annual Leave) (Amendment) Regulations 2018 which came into force on the 6th April 2020) must be given to employees on or before their first day of employment.

EMPLOYMENT CONTRACT FOR HOMEWORKERS ('this document')

From: *[name of employer] [address]* ('we' 'us' or 'the Company')

To: [name of employee] [address] ('you')

1. General

The following particulars are given to you in accordance with the Employment Rights Act 1996 (as amended).

1.2 You agree to all the terms and conditions set out in this document.

1.3 This document annuls any previous agreement whether spoken or written given to you at any time.

2. Job title

You are employed as a *[job title]*. But you agree to work in any other role reasonably within your capabilities.

3. Line manager

Your current line manager is *[name and/or job title]*, but any other manager or person in authority may give you work instructions, and should be contacted by you as and when necessary if your line manager is unavailable.

4. Continuous employment

4.1 Your period of continuous employment with us began on the *[date]*.

4.2 No employment with a previous employer counts as part of your period of continuous employment.

OR

4.2 Your employment with *[name of previous employer]* which began on the *[date]* will count as part of your continuous period of employment with us.

5. Probationary period

5.1 As you are a new employee, the first *[number]* month*[s]* of your employment shall be a probationary period and your employment may be terminated during this period at any time on *[one week's]* prior notice. We may, at our discretion, extend this probationary period for up to a further *[number]* months. During this probationary period the homeworking arrangements and your performance and suitability for continued employment will be monitored. At the end of your probationary period you will be informed in writing if you have successfully completed your probationary period and if the homeworking arrangements are considered appropriate for your continued employment.

OR

5.1 As you are an existing employee, who has been employed previously at our business premises, the first *[number]* month*[s]* of the homeworking arrangements described in this document shall be a trial period. We may, at our discretion, extend this trial period for up to a further *[number]* months. During this trial period the homeworking arrangements will be monitored. At the end of the trial period you will be informed in writing if the homeworking arrangements are considered appropriate or whether such arrangements should be terminated in accordance with the next clause.

5.2 If, at any time during or at the end of the *[probationary]* OR *[trial]* period, the Company considers the homeworking arrangements to be unsatisfactory or the requirements of the business change such that homeworking is no longer appropriate, we may give you *[number]* [*days'* OR *weeks'* OR *months'*] notice to change your place of work to the Company's premises at *[address]* and return to any previous terms and conditions of employment in existence immediately before this document was agreed.

6. Place of work

6.1 Your normal place of work will be *[home address]*. You are required to inform us as soon as possible if you decide to change your home address.

6.2 You may be required from time to time to make business visits and/or work at such other locations and for such times as we may request.

[6.3 In the course of your duties you may also be required to make business visits throughout the UK and abroad.]

7. Prohibition

You confirm that you are not prohibited from working from your home by any covenant or restriction in any document which is legally enforceable by a third party.

8. Collective agreements

There are no collective agreements relevant to your employment.

9. Remuneration

9.1 You will be paid *[weekly]* OR *[monthly]* by credit transfer to your Bank account in arrears at the rate of £*[amount]* gross each *[week]* OR *[month]* (and proportionately for any lesser period, each pay instalment being deemed to accrue rateably from day to day).

9.2 Your salary will be reviewed annually entirely at our discretion.

10. Hours of work

10.1 Your normal weekly hours will be *[number]* hours to be worked at such times as are necessary for the effective performance of your duties. You must be available for work and contactable during these hours.

10.2 In addition, you will be required to be available at home at such times as we may reasonably request.

10.3 In certain circumstances it may be necessary to adjust or exceed your hours of work in order to ensure that your job duties are properly performed.

10.4 Any overtime or excess hours that you work will be unpaid unless payment is agreed and authorised in writing by your line manager before you do the extra work.

10.5 You are entitled to a rest break of 20 minutes for every 6 hours that you work. It is your responsibility to ensure you take this rest break.

11. Incapacity

11.1 In the event that you are unable to work for a medical or any other reason you should contact your line manager as soon as possible.

11.2 A failure to contact the Company, without a good reason, regarding your incapacity to work, may be investigated.

11.3 If the incapacity is due to sickness a self-certification form must be completed within 7 days from the commencement of the period of incapacity. The form will be supplied to you by your line manager.

11.4 A medical certificate signed by your doctor (know as a 'fit note') as to the reason for the incapacity must be sent to the

Company if you are medically incapacitated for any period of 7 consecutive days or more. A new medical certificate should be sent thereafter periodically as required by the Company.

11.5 For the purposes of the Statutory Sick Pay scheme the agreed 'qualifying days' are Monday to Friday.

11.6 You have no contractual right to be paid your salary in respect of periods of incapacity.

12. Holidays

12.1 You are entitled to the following paid holidays:

12.1.1 The 8 statutory holidays, which are New Year's Day, Good Friday, Easter Monday, May Day, Spring Bank Holiday, Late Summer Bank Holiday, Christmas Day and Boxing Day; plus

12.1.2 *[number]* days' holiday in each holiday year, pro rata if you work part-time.

12.1.3 If you are required to work on one of the statutory holidays you will be given another day's holiday in lieu

12.2 Holidays must be agreed with your line manager before you book the holiday.

12.3. The holiday year is the calendar year from *[start date]* to *[end date]* and you should take your holidays during this period. You will not be permitted to carry over unused holiday entitlement into a following holiday year except with the Company's express consent or as may be permitted by law.

12.4 You may not take as holiday more than *[10]* working days consecutively out of your holiday entitlement without the agreement of your line manager.

12.5 You will be paid for any outstanding holiday entitlement you may have as at the date your employment ends.

12.6 If, when your employment ends, you have taken more than your holiday entitlement for the current holiday year then a sum equivalent to wages for the additional holiday taken will be deducted from any final payment due to you.

13. Pension

Written details of any pension scheme applicable to you are available from your line manager.

14. Termination of employment

14.1 During any probationary period the notice required by either of us to terminate your employment will be one week.

14.2 At the end of any probationary period, the notice required by either of us to terminate your employment will be the statutory minimum which is:

- one week's notice if you have been continuously employed for up to 2 years; and then
- one week's notice for each completed year of employment from 2 completed years up to a maximum of 12 weeks' notice.

14.3 We reserve the right to pay you salary in lieu of notice.

14.4 Nothing in the document prevents us from terminating your employment summarily or otherwise in the event of any serious breach by you of the terms herein or in the event of any act or acts of gross misconduct by you.

14.5 On the termination of your employment you will be required to return to the Company all documents and electronic and other equipment in your possession belonging to, or relating to, the Company's business.

15. Company Property

15.1 We shall provide you with the following property and equipment, collectively referred to as 'Company Property' to enable you to do your job:

[PROPERTY AND EQUIPMENT TO BE PROVIDED].

15.2 For the avoidance of doubt, the Company Property shall remain the property of the Company and you shall not permit use of it by any person other than yourself and any other person duly authorised by the Company.

15.3 We shall install, service and maintain the Company Property as necessary.

15.4 You shall be responsible for any damage to the Company Property which goes beyond ordinary wear and tear. You are required to report to the Company any such damage or malfunction of the Company Property as soon as you become aware of it.

15.5 We shall be responsible for taking out and maintaining a valid policy of insurance covering the Company Property against fire, theft, loss and damage throughout your employment, in so far as such property is not covered by an insurance policy taken out by you. We will give you any necessary information to enable you to comply with this clause.

15.6 You shall not do, cause or permit any act or omission which will invalidate any insurance policy covering the Company Property.

16. Right to enter

You consent to the Company's representatives, at reasonable times and on reasonable notice, entering your home address to:

- install, inspect, replace, repair, maintain or service the Company Property during your employment;
- carry out health and safety risk assessments of the Company Property and your workstation during your employment;
- recover the Company Property on or after termination of your employment; and
- monitor the work you are doing.

17. Visiting your home

We reserve the right to visit you at home at agreed times for work-related purposes, including health and safety matters. It is a condition of this homeworking agreement that you agree to accept visits from us in your home. Such visits may include for the purposes of:

- confirming suitability of the home working environment;
- delivering and collecting work;
- providing a channel for reporting;
- general discussions about work-related matters;
- ensuring health, safety, wellbeing and security;
- any other work-related purposes that we consider appropriate.

18. Household expenses

It is not Company policy to pay or contribute towards household expenses incurred by a homeworker even when such expenses are increased by the work done for the Company by the homeworker.

19. Grievance procedures

This grievance procedure is not contractual and the Company reserves the right to change it or to deviate from it for any reason.

- If you have a grievance or complaint to do with your work or the people you work with you should, whenever possible, discuss the matter informally with your line manager. You may be able to agree a solution informally between you.
- If the matter is serious and/or you wish to raise the matter formally you should set out your grievance(s) in writing to your line manager.
- If your grievance is against your line manager, or you feel unable to approach him or her for any reason, you should talk to another manager.
- The manager who is dealing with your grievance will arrange a meeting with you, normally within 5 days, to discuss your grievance(s). You have the right to be accompanied by a work colleague of your choice or trade union representative at this meeting if you make a reasonable request. After the meeting the manager will give you a decision in writing, normally within one working day.
- If you are unhappy with the manager's decision and you wish to appeal you should set out the reasons in writing addressed to the manager who will arrange for another

manager to hear your appeal. Your appeal will be heard by the different manager, normally within 5 days. You have the right to be accompanied by a work colleague of your choice or trade union representative at the appeal-meeting if you make a reasonable request. After the meeting the manager who heard your appeal will give you a decision, normally within one working day.
- The appeal decision is final.

20. Disciplinary procedures

The disciplinary rules applicable to your employment are set out in the current Staff Handbook, a copy of which you should have received. (contact your line manager if you do not have a copy).

21. Confidentiality

You shall not during or after your employment with us disclose confidential information belonging to the Company. You have a personal responsibility to protect and maintain confidentiality of both Company and client information. You must not, except as authorised by the Company or required by law or by your job duties, reveal any of the Company's confidential information. This obligation will continue after the termination of your employment unless and until any such information comes into the public domain other than through any breach of this provision by you. You may be required as a condition of your continued employment with us to sign an express confidentiality undertaking. GDPR principles also apply to homeworkers and must be followed at all times. Please be mindful of our GDPR Policy document.

22. Confidential information in your home

You are responsible for ensuring the security of confidential information in your home. In particular, you undertake to:

- encrypt and/or protect by a strong password any confidential information held on your home computer;
- lock your computer terminal whenever it is left unattended;
- ensure any wireless network used is secure;
- keep all papers containing confidential information in filing cabinets that are locked when not in use; and
- comply with the Company's data protection policy from time to time in force regarding the retention of personal data.

23. Monitoring

23.1 The Company reserves the right to monitor, to a reasonable extent and by reasonable means, the work done by you in the course of your employment with the Company.

23.2 Monitoring may be by software programs installed on any computer, mobile phone or electronic equipment belonging to the Company and used by you in the course of your employment with the Company.

23.3 Monitoring may also include an examination of all data on any Company computer or mobile phone that you use. An examination of data may take place at your home or remotely.

23.4 By signing this document you consent to the reasonable monitoring by the Company of the work you do in the course of your employment as a homeworker.

24. Internet Policy

24.1 You are reminded that the Company's Internet Policy also applies to homeworkers and prohibits employees using Company computers or mobile phones to access websites other than in the course of their employment.

24.2 Also, the Internet Policy warns that employees must not send, on behalf of the Company or otherwise, any email or electronic communication which could be considered illegal, offensive or defamatory or which could bring the Company into disrepute or cause legal action to be taken against the Company.

24.3 Further, employees must not open emails or electronic communications from unknown senders or download any new software onto a Company computer or mobile phone without the permission of their line manager.

[24.4 The Company's Policies, including the Internet Policy, are on the Company's intranet to which you have access.]

25. Deductions from pay

The Company reserves the right to deduct from your pay any monies owing by you to the Company if the said deduction is permitted by law. By signing this document you consent to and authorise the Company to make any appropriate deduction(s).

26. Lay offs and short-time working

26.1 Although every reasonable effort will always be made to ensure full employment, in the event of a temporary shortage of work the Company reserves the right to temporarily lay-off or place on short-time working any employees affected.

26.2 If you are laid off or are placed on short working you will have certain statutory rights in connection with the lay-off. Please ask your line manager for more information.

27. Training

At the beginning of your employment you will be given training appropriate to your job duties and job experience. You will not be contractually entitled to any other training, but if the need for further training arises, this will be provided to you on terms and conditions to be discussed and agreed with you at the relevant time.

28. Benefits

For the avoidance of doubt, during your employment with the Company, you will not entitled to any benefits other than those benefits which are set out in this document, or as may be set out in a job-offer letter (if you received one) or in the Staff Handbook or in a stand-alone Policy document (for example, a Maternity Policy). If you have a query as to your possible entitlement to a specific benefit or benefits please raise the query in writing with your line manager.

29. Changes to this document

The Company reserves the right to review, revise, amend or replace the content of this employment contract and introduce new terms and conditions from time to time or to vary existing terms and conditions to reflect the changing needs of the business and to comply with new legislation.

30. Contract of Employment

By signing below you confirm that you accept this document (plus any additional terms in a job-offer letter) as your contract of employment, and you agree to comply with the work rules set out in the Staff Handbook and to comply with our stand-alone Policies. You acknowledge that you have been given a copy of the Staff Handbook and that you may obtain any Policy from your line manager as and when the Policy is relevant to you.

Signed:

Dated:

(for and on behalf of the employer)

Signed:

Dated:

(employee)

Homeworking Policy

You may use the draft Homeworking Policy below in your business. An editable copy in RTF format can be downloaded from: https://worklaw.co.uk/homeworkers.html.

However, please remember that the document was not drafted specifically for your business and may not be entirely suitable for your business. Probably it will need amending.

Worklaw (https://worklaw.co.uk/employmentcontracts.php) can draft a Homeworking Employment Contract and a Homeworking Policy specifically for your business for a total fee of £198. This fee also includes advice on employment law by email or telephone for one month from the date we received payment of our fee.

It is not mandatory to have a written Homeworking Policy but it generally makes sense for the employer to have one, particularly in the event of a dispute with the employee over some aspect of homeworking.

HOMEWORKING POLICY

Introduction

1.1 This Policy is not contractual and we reserve the right, at our absolute discretion and at any time, to withdraw this Policy or change or delete any term in this Policy or to add a term to this Policy.

1.2 Homeworking is an option we endeavour to make available to all employees.

1.3 We define 'homeworking' as when our employee's normal place of work is their home either on a permanent basis or on a temporary basis.

1.4 The reference in this policy to a 'line manager' is intended to include any other manager or person in the business with authority to give you work-instructions.

1.5 Employees working from home will be expected to attend meetings and other office-based events as and when required by their line manager.

1.6 Employees working from home are required to comply with Company policies, including holiday, performance targets, sickness absences, other absences etc.

Permanent or regular homeworking

2.1 We define 'permanent' as being when the employee regularly works from home for all or most of their working week but makes occasional visits to the office or to other work-locations as required by the needs of the business.

2.2 The homeworking arrangement is also considered to be permanent if the employee regularly works a defined part of their working week at home but regularly works the other working days of the week in the office, for example, they regularly work from home a set 3 days each week but work the other 2 days in the office.

Temporary or occasional homeworking

3.1 We define 'temporary' as when the employee works from home occasionally, as and when required by the needs of the business, or if they make a request to work from home on a particular day, or part of a day, and we agree to the request.

3.2 Temporary homeworking may be agreed between us in relation to specific tasks or job duties or for specific periods, without a regular pattern.

3.3 Homeworking may also be agreed as part of a phased return to work after maternity or sickness absence, or be a temporary arrangement due to family commitments or domestic circumstances.

4. Employment contracts

4.1 Some new employees are engaged on the basis that they work all their contracted hours from home.

4.2 Some existing employees may be offered the opportunity to work from home if their job duties can be performed as efficiently from home as from an office.

4.3 We reserve the right to decide whether homeworking is suitable. Employment contracts will confirm that we reserve the right to withdraw or change the homeworking arrangements at our absolute discretion.

4.4 If there is a conflict between anything written in an employment contract and anything written in this Policy, it is the employment contract which applies.

5. Homeworking request by you

5.1 Our approval must be sought before you may work from home.

5.2 Existing employees are entitled to apply to work from home on a permanent basis or on a temporary basis.

5.3 Applications for homeworking on a permanent basis must be made formally in writing to your line manager, stating the working

pattern requested with all relevant information to support the application. Relevant information is likely to include:
- the date on which the homeworking should start;
- the number of days each week you propose to work from home;
- whether your proposed hours will be fixed (that is, will not change from week to week) or be flexible
- where in your home you intend to work;
- what equipment you have to enable you to work from home;
- what equipment will need to be provided;
- who else will be in your home during our working hours;
- the arrangement you will make to secure business equipment and confidential documents.

5.4 Applications by you for homeworking on a temporary basis may be made to your line manager on a less formal basis than that required for permanent home working, as long as you make clear the reason for the application.

5.5 Requests by you for homeworking will be considered and will be approved at the line manager's discretion, taking into account your job role and the needs of the business, and in particular, whether they work you are employed to do can be done, without significant difficulty, from a private household.

5.6 The factors taken into account your personal suitability for home working are likely to include an assessment of your:
- skills and attributes;

- likely degree of self-discipline;
- ability to work without direct supervision;
- organisational skills;
- ability to manage time effectively;
- ability to cope with the potentially conflicting demands of your work and your household.

5.7 A review will also be made as to whether your home contains suitable space for home working.

5.8 The homeworking arrangement must be cost-effective and must not cause a significant increase in the workload on any of your work-colleagues or on management.

5.9 We reserve the right to refuse your application for home working or to grant your application subject to conditions.

5.10 Each application will be viewed and decided on its own merits; the fact that a similar application was granted in the past is not a factor which will taken into account.

5.11 Employees who work from home will be expected to make themselves available outside their normal or agreed hours of work, on being given reasonable notice.

5.12 Employees working from home will be expected to attend meetings and other office-based events as and when required by their line manager.

6. Homeworking requests by the Company

If we have reasons to ask you to work from home, either on a permanent or a temporary basis, you do not need to agree if you do not wish to do so, and you will not need to give a reason for your refusal and you will not suffer a detriment or be penalised in any way if you refuse. We wish to make clear that working from home is entirely voluntary on the part of the employee.

7. Criteria

All requests by existing employees for homeworking will be reviewed on their merit and all job roles will be subject to relevant criteria to make sure the job is suitable for homeworking. Relevant criteria includes whether the nature of the work will benefit from peace and quiet and a lack of interruptions.

8. Trial period

8.1 Normally, homeworking arrangements will be subject to a trial 3-month period to assess that working from home is suitable for the job role.

8.2 The trial period will be confirmed in writing with any other terms and conditions relevant to homeworking.

8.3 During the trial period you may may make suggestions as to how the homeworking arrangements might be improved.

8.4 If the home working arrangements continue after the trial period has expired, the arrangements will be reviewed periodically.

9. Grievances

If you feel that we have been unreasonable in the way we have dealt with your application for homeworking, you are reminded that you may raise a grievance using our formal grievance procedure which is set out in your employment contract.

10. Appeals

10.1 If your application for home working is refused we will explain why in writing and you may appeal this decision.

10.2 If a homeworking arrangement is withdrawn, after the trial period, or at any other time, we will explain why in writing and you may appeal this decision.

10.3 The grounds of appeal must be in writing and submitted to the manager who took the decision to refuse the application, usually within 5 working days of the decision.

10.4 Any appeal will be heard by another manager, not previously involved in the situation, and you will have a right to be accompanied by a work colleague or a trade union representative if you are in that union at any appeal hearing.

11. Flexible working

You may have a statutory right to request flexible working as an alternative to homeworking. If you are interested in flexible working, and if you do not have a copy already, please ask your line manager for a copy of our Flexible Working Policy which sets out the relevant qualification criteria and the procedure which applies.

12. Induction

During their induction, new employees will be informed that homeworking might be viable possibility for them depending on the requirements of the job they have been employed to do.

13. Company Equipment

13.1 In the event that homeworking arrangements are agreed, and depending on your job role, it is likely that we will need to provide you with some or all of the equipment listed below, or reimburse you the relevant expenditure if you pay for any of the items listed, which we refer to as 'Company equipment'.

13.2 Company equipment is likely to comprise the following (the list is not exhaustive)

- dedicated work phone, with answering machine (landline and mobile or both)
- laptop or desktop computer (or both);
- printer;
- scanner;
- shredder;
- filing cabinet with locks for confidential documents;
- modem;
- work desk;
- adequate lighting system;
- adjustable chair (with lumbar support);
- stationery;
- cleaning materials;
- first aid kit;
- smoke detector;
- fire extinguisher;
- safety equipment, such as surge protectors;
- burglar alarm system;
- any other necessary equipment not listed above.

13.3 For the avoidance of doubt, all Company equipment remains the property of the Company irrespective of the length of time the equipment is in your possession. Also, if you purchased the equipment but were reimbursed in full the cost you paid, for the avoidance of doubt, the equipment became the property of the Company as at the date you were reimbursed in full.

13.4 You must keep all Company equipment in reasonable condition and secure.

13.5 You must notify the Company if any equipment is damaged or fails.

13.6 The Company reserves the right to attend your home to check, update, maintain or repair or replace the equipment, on giving you reasonable notice.

13.7 The use, including personal use, of all Company equipment must be in accordance with the Staff Handbook and any relevant stand-alone Policy; for example, you must not use a Company laptop to access gambling sites as this is prohibited by the Company's Internet Policy.

13.8 You must not allow any other person in your home to use Company equipment without the written permission of your line manager.

13.9 You must not allow any person in your home to read or access or take copies of any Company document, even if the document is not regarded as confidential.

14. Household expenses

As stated in your employment contract it is not generally Company policy to pay or contribute towards household expenses incurred by a homeworker even when such expenses are increased by the work done for the Company by the homeworker.

In special circumstances, the Company might agree to pay or

contribute towards increased household expenses, but only if such an agreement is incorporated in a separate document signed by the Company and by you following professional advice from a suitably qualified accountant as to the tax implications of such payments.

15. Health and safety

15.1 As an employer we are responsible employer for ensuring, so far as it is reasonably practical, the health, safety and welfare at work of all employees. This responsibility also applies to employees who work from home. Therefore, we reserve the right, to visit you at home periodically to check that your working environment complies with all aspects of relevant health and safety legislation. We will give you reasonable notice of such a visit. We envisage 'reasonable notice' to be, at least one week's notice, except in an emergency.

15.2 As the control that we can exercise over employees working from home is limited, the onus is also on you to ensure that you, and members of your household, and visitors to your home, are not endangered by the work you do at home.

15.3 Employees who work from home must ensure they have a suitable environment where they can focus on work.

15.4 If you think any aspect of working from home is affecting your health you must inform your line manager as soon as possible in order that any appropriate measures are taken.

15.5 The Company's Health and Safety Policy and the sections on health and safety in the Staff Handbook also apply to homeworkers.

16. Sickness absence

Homeworkers must comply with our sickness absence procedure which is referred to in their employment contract and in the staff handbook, and report their incapacity for work to their line manager when they are sick and unable to work.

17. Risk Assessments

17. 1 The Company reserves the right to carry out periodic risk assessments to identify any relevant risks and to prevent harm to the homeworker or anyone else who may be affected by their work. The Company may need to check such workplaces from time to time as the homeworking arrangement proceeds.

17.2 Homeworkers must contact their line manager immediately they identify a risk or a potential risk of any sort caused by their work.

17.3 If you are disabled we will carry out an assessment to ascertain whether reasonable adjustments can and should be made in your home to assist you in your work.

18. Accidents

Homeworkers must notify the Company if they suffer an accident or injury in the course of their employment in accordance with the Company's Health and Safety Policy.

19. Safe use of equipment

19.1 Homeworkers must use all electrical and other equipment safely and in accordance with best practice and manufacturer's guidelines.

19.2 The Company reserves the right to check all Company

electrical equipment in the home for safety, including electrical sockets and wiring.

20. Pregnancy

Homeworkers who are pregnant, or who have someone in their household who is pregnant, must notify the Company of the pregnancy and the Company will carry out a risk assessment in relation to the pregnancy.

21. Informing authorities

If legislation requires, employees who work from home must take responsibility for informing HMRC and their local authority and any other relevant authority, that their home is being used partly for business.

22. Tax

Employees who work from home are responsible for checking with an accountant (or HMRC) that there are no adverse tax implications caused by homeworking, for example, capital gains tax. In the event that tax is payable due to homeworking, for the avoidance of doubt, this will be the responsibility of the employee and the employer will not contribute.

23. Home insurance

Employees who work from home must check that working from home is permitted by any insurance policy affecting their home. We reserve the right to see and keep a copy of the relevant policy.

24. Reviews

24.1 We reserve the right to review any existing homeworking arrangements and thereafter to withdraw or change the arrangements as we decide. In particular, a home working arrangement is likely to be withdrawn or changed if the employee is underperforming or the needs of the business are not being met.

24.2 Under normal circumstances, and in the absence of an emergency, the employee will be given at least a week's notice that we intend to review their home working arrangements.

24.3 A review will include at least one meeting between the employee and their line manager, either at an agreed venue or electronically, when all the relevant facts and paperwork will be discussed and considered before any decision is made.

24.4 The employee will be given at least a week's notice, following the relevant meeting with their line manager, if our decision is to withdraw or vary the home working arrangement. The reasons for any withdrawal and change will be set out in writing. The employee will the have one week from receipt of the written reasons in which to appeal against the decision. If they so wish, the employee is entitled to have a work colleague of their choice or a trade union official if they are in that union, with them at the appeal as their companion. The employee may raise a formal grievance using the Grievance Procedure.

25. Data protection

25.1 Employees working from home are responsible for complying with data protection law and for keeping all business documents and information secure at all times.

25.2 You must encrypt and protect all electronic data pertaining to the Company by strong passwords (at least 15 characters), which should be changed regularly (at least every 3 months);

25.3 You must not download any new software onto a Company computer or mobile phone without the permission of your line manager.

25.4 You must lock your computer(s) whenever left unattended.

25.5 You must not open any email which is from an unknown source or otherwise suspicious.

25.6 You must not give any information about the Company or your work to any person who is unknown to you. Instead, you must refer that person to your line manager.

25.7 All employees must comply with our Data Protection Policy (a copy is available from your line manager if you do not have a copy).

26. Travel expenses

Homeworkers, who are required by their job-duties to attend meetings, away from their workplace at home, will be reimbursed their reasonable travel expenses in accordance with the Company's Expenses Policy. Ask your line manager for a copy of this Policy *[which is also on the Company's intranet]*.

27. Use of own vehicle

A homeworker may use their own vehicle for business purposes only if the use is in accordance with our Company Vehicle Policy. Ask your line manager for a copy of this Policy *[which is also on the Company's intranet]*.

28. Revealing personal information

Unless necessary in the course of their employment and job duties, employees working from home should not provide third parties (which includes customers or clients) with their home address and personal contact details. If possible, contact with third parties should be routed through the Company's offices.

29. Business meetings

Employees working from home should not hold meetings with customers or clients at their home unless this cannot be avoided. Whenever possible, business meeting should take place at the Company's workplace or at another suitable venue such as a hotel with business-meeting rooms.

30. Moving home

If homeworkers move home, the homeworking arrangement may be reassessed. If the Company considers that the change of home would make, or has made, homeworking unsuitable, this may result in the homeworking arrangement coming to an end.

31. Monitoring

As stated in your Employment Contract, the Company reserves the right to monitor the work done by you in the course of your employment by all reasonable means, including electronic surveillance.

32. Hours

You must record in writing, electronically or in print, how long you spend each day working for the Company as we need to monitor the number of hours you work each day for the purposes of the Working Time regulations to ensure that you do not exceed 48 hours a week averaged over a 17-week period. If you are likely to exceed the hours permitted by the Working Time regulations please inform us and we will take the necessary measures to ensure that we comply with the regulations.

33. Smoking

You must not smoke while you are working if more than one person is working with you or if a customer or client or third party visits you at home in the course of your employment.

34. Contact

You must inform your line manager if you feel you are not coping with any aspect of your work when working from home. Everything you say to your line manager will be treated in confidence unless he or she has your express permission to disclose what you say to other persons. We are here to help you.

35. Other clauses

[*Please add any other clauses which are relevant to your particular business, or delete clause in this draft which are not relevant*].

Bullet Point Booklets

1. Disciplinary Procedures
2. National Minimum Wage
3. Employment Contracts
4. Defending Employment Tribunal Claims
5. TUPE
6. Staff Handbooks
7. Disability Discrimination
8. Settlement Agreements

9. Redundancy

10. Recruitment

11. Sick Pay

12. Maternity

13. Homeworking (this booklet)

Printed in Great Britain
by Amazon